Gidget
the
Surfing
Dog

Featuring photography by

Charmaine Gray

Mike Barton, Fiona Kempin, Dominique Labrecque,

Dale Porter, and Chris Stone

Manufactured in China by C&C Offset Printing Co. Ltd.
Shenzhen, Guangdong Province, in December 2019

LITTLE BIGFOOT with colophon is a registered trademark of Penguin Random House LLC

24 23 22 21 20   9 8 7 6 5 4 3 2 1

Editor: Christy Cox
Production editor: Bridget Sweet
Design: Tony Ong

Photo editor: Karin Anderson
Cover photograph: Charmaine Gray Photography
Illustrations: Susanna Ryan

Interior photographs: Mike Barton (pages 2–3, 20—center/bottom, 22–23, 33—left, 34—bottom, 36, and 39), Charmaine Gray Photography (pages 11—top, 14–15, 20—top, 25–26, 28—right, 29—right, 30, 32, 33—right, 34—top, 35, 44—top, 45—left/bottom, and 48), Fiona Kempin (pages 16 and 41), Dominique Labrecque (pages 11—bottom, 17, 28—left, 29—left, 33—bottom, 37, and 44—bottom), courtesy of Alecia Nelson (pages 4-9, 27, 31, and 42), Dale Porter/DogTog.com (pages 12 and 24—bottom), Chris Stone (pages 1, 10, 24—top, 38, 40, 45—top, and 46—bottom), and Wikimedia Commons (page 43). Back cover photographs: background photo by Dominique Labrecque and smaller photos courtesy of Alecia Nelson.

Photographers retain all rights to their photos.

Library of Congress Cataloging-in-Publication Data

Names: Rusch, Elizabeth, author.
Title: Gidget the surfing dog : catching waves with a small but mighty pug / [Elizabeth Rusch].
Description: Seattle, WA : Little Bigfoot, [2020] | Includes bibliographical references. | Audience: Ages: 7-10 | Audience: Grades: 2-3 |
Identifiers: LCCN 2019024922 | ISBN 9781632172716 (hardcover)
Subjects: LCSH: Gidget (Dog)--Juvenile literature. | Dogs--United States--Biography--Juvenile literature. | Surfing--United States--Juvenile literature. | Pug--Behavior--Juvenile literature.
Classification: LCC SF426.5 .R86 2020 | DDC 636.70092/9--dc23
LC record available at https://lccn.loc.gov/2019024922

ISBN: 978-1-63217-271-6

Sasquatch Books
1904 Third Avenue, Suite 710
Seattle, WA 98101
SasquatchBooks.com

GIDGET THE SURFING DOG

Catching Waves with a Small but Mighty Pug

Elizabeth Rusch

little bigfoot
an imprint of sasquatch books
seattle, wa

Izzy

Gidget

All Alecia Nelson wanted was a friend for her dog, Izzy. "What I got was a little terror," she says.

Most pugs are not particularly athletic. But Gidget sprinted, climbed, and leapt all over the house.

Most pugs don't fetch, but Gidget chased balls for hours.

Most pugs tire easily. But Gidget was an endless bundle of energy, zooming around like a bug in a jar and gnawing on a brand-new leather couch.

"Gidget was so hyper, my furniture and floors were getting trashed," Alecia says. "I didn't know what to do."

So Alecia got goats. Gidget chased them around the yard and bounced in the air with joy. Her new friends took the edge off. But it wasn't enough. "I racked my brain about how to manage this little fireball," Alecia says.

Goat

Izzy

Keep the Pug Busy

Alecia tried dog agility. She and her energetic pug spent hours together learning commands and mastering obstacles. Following Alecia's pointed finger, Gidget vaulted over gates like a racehorse, burrowed through tunnels like a prairie dog, and scrambled up and down ladders like her goat friends. "But the sport was so hard on her limbs," Alecia says. "I worried it would wear out her little body."

While Izzy was more of a homebody, Gidget wanted to go with Alecia everywhere. In the winter, Alecia plopped Gidget on a sled. The pug rode the whole way down—standing up!

In the summer, Alecia brought her along on her stand-up paddleboard.

Most pugs hate the water. But Gidget splashed about while Alecia got the board ready.

Most pugs don't swim. But Gidget doggie-paddled happily in her little life jacket.

Most pugs don't balance on boards. But Gidget took to the board like she was born for it, chilling out even in the roughest waters.

How Does a Surfboard Float?

Any object in water is pulled downward by gravity and pushed upward from a force called buoyancy. As an object pushes down on the water, the water pushes back. The more water an object displaces (or pushes away), the stronger the force of buoyancy. A small, dense object like a rock sinks in water because the pull of gravity is stronger than the force of the small amount of displaced water. A long, flat, broad object like a surfboard displaces much more water, so the force of buoyancy overcomes the force of gravity—keeping the board afloat.

Dogs Surf?

One day, Alecia and Gidget chanced upon a dog surfing contest at their favorite dog beach. Del Mar in California was alive with dogs of all breeds—goldens, mastiffs, doodles, boxers, min pins, and mutts. At the blare of a horn, a pack of dogs and people bounded into the surf.

After battling through the breakers, the dogs settled on boards and their owners launched them onto waves. Some pups surfed sitting down, some surfed standing up, and some surfed in a crouch with their butts up in the air. Lots of dogs wobbled and fell off. *Gidgie could do this*, thought Alecia, who grew up surfing. *Her balance is incredible.*

Take a Break

There are three main kinds of surfable wave breaks:

Reef Breaks

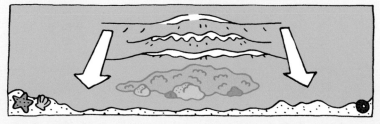

Reef breaks form when waves rise up over an underwater coral or rock reef, often far from shore. The break is limited to the length of the reef.

Point Breaks

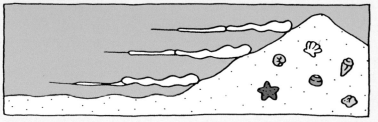

Point breaks form when waves wrap around a point or headland and then curl and break as they run along the coastline. Point breaks often offer the longest rides.

Beach Breaks

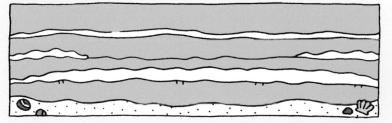

Beach breaks form when waves drag on the sand near shore, curling and breaking along the length of a sandbar or along the beach. Most dog surfing happens at beach breaks.

A week later, the pair gave surfing a try. Alecia strapped Gidget into her life jacket, plopped her onto a small surfboard, and pushed her out through the waves. Their friend Fiona waited closer to shore.

As a small swell glided toward them, Alecia spoke calmly and cheerfully to Gidget: "You're OK."

When the wave was about to hit, she cooed: "Here we go."

And she launched the pug in front of the wave.

All About Wind and Waves

Making Waves

Swells are formed far away, when wind blows across the surface of the ocean and friction from the wind pushes the water. The weird thing about waves is that the water doesn't travel with the wave—only the energy travels. The wind forces the molecules of water to move in a circular motion. So while the energy of the swell moves across the ocean, the water molecules themselves travel in circles, returning to the same place.

Breaking Waves

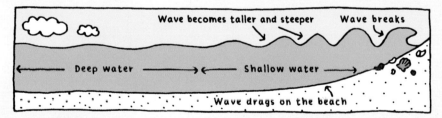

When a swell nears shore, the bottom of the wave drags along the ocean floor and slows. The top of the wave continues at the same speed and eventually tilts forward, curls over, and creates a breaker.

Shaping Waves

Wind not only forms swells off in the distance; it can also affect the shape of the waves near shore. Surfers pay close attention to the wind direction, especially onshore and offshore winds.

ONSHORE WINDS

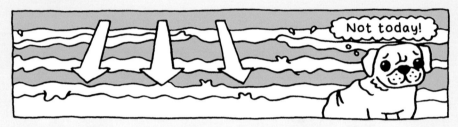

Winds that blow from the ocean toward the beach often create choppy, bumpy, unstable swells. Some waves are still rideable.

OFFSHORE WINDS

Winds that blow from the beach out to sea often push onto the face of the waves, creating clean, tall waves that break more slowly and give a longer, smoother ride.

Gidget and the board disappeared behind a wall of water. Alecia rushed toward the beach to see what would happen. The pug glided right by Fiona and surfed all the way to shore.

But before Alecia and Fiona had a moment to think, Gidget leapt off the board and took off running across the sand.

Was the little pug terrified?

But Gidget wasn't running away. She ran in a big circle—a victory lap. Then she sprinted back to her board, hopped on, and barked out *woo, woo, woo!* She couldn't wait to go again.

Can Your Dog Hang Ten?

Before introducing any dog to surfing, make sure you have experience and confidence in the waves as a surfer or boogie boarder. Then make sure your dog enjoys playing in the water and the waves. Throw a ball or stick in ankle-deep water and watch the dog's reaction. If they avoid the water or seem fearful, they will probably not enjoy the sport.

Let your dog get accustomed to standing on the surfboard on the beach. Before hitting the waves, put the dog in a doggie life jacket. Small dogs or breeds sensitive to cold may need wet suits made especially for dogs or adapted from a human wet suit.

Start with small waves close to shore. Settle your dog on the board and push the board in front of a wave. Look for these clues that your dog is relaxed and enjoying the ride:

- The dog moves calmly on the board.
- Their ears are up or floppy.
- The dog sits or stands rather than cowers. (A crouch position is fine as long as the ears are up and the dog looks relaxed.)

Watch what happens when the board reaches the beach. Does the dog seem eager for more?

Types of Waves

Surging Breakers

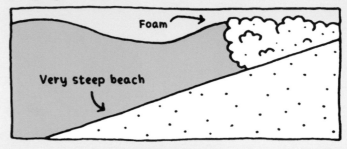

On very steep beaches, these waves rise up and smash down suddenly, creating an undertow as the water drains back quickly.

Closeouts

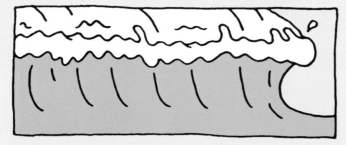

These are waves that break all at once from end to end. They don't offer a tube or a gradually breaking wave face to surf along.

Spilling Breakers

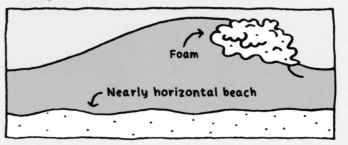

On flat beaches, the crest of the wave spills raggedly over the wave face.

Reform

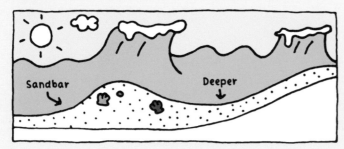

A breaker that hits an area of deeper water, losing its shape, and then hits shallower water and reforms again.

Plunging Breakers

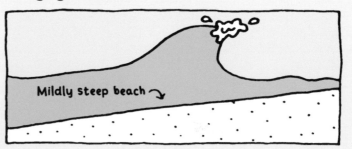

On mildly steep beaches, the waves rise up smoothly, creating a concave shape called a hollow, barrel, or tube. Surfers love to tuck into and ride inside these tubes, which they call the green room.

Rights/Lefts

Waves that start to break at one point and peel to the left or the right. A surfer rides at an angle, staying in front of the peeling break.

A-Frame

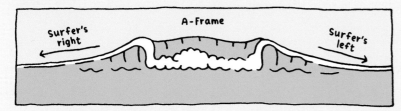

Surfing waves that start at a point and peel to the left and to the right. Two surfers can catch the same wave, moving away from each other.

Double-Up

When two waves meet, their troughs and crests align, creating a large and powerful wave from their combined energy. Sometimes called sneaker waves, these oversized waves pack a punch much greater than other waves hitting the beach around the same time.

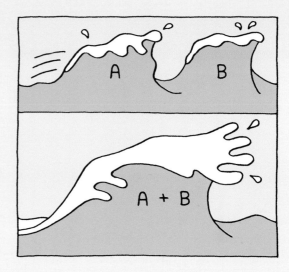

Wave Parts

Science Terms

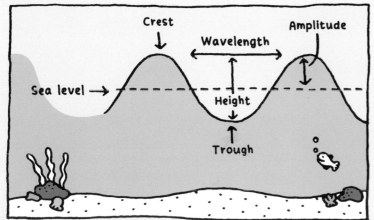

Surfing Terms

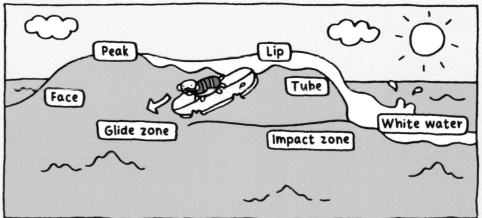

The Search for the Perfect Wave

Alecia and Gidget started surfing regularly. Since Gidget can't pick a wave or paddle herself in front of it, choosing a wave is Alecia's job. It's one part luck, two parts skill. "I'm looking for a wave that will break evenly from the top down, peeling off to one or both sides," says Alecia. She avoids closeouts, when the whole wave front crashes at once.

When Alecia spots a promising wave, she turns Gidget's board toward the beach. Placement on the face of the wave has to be just right. Alecia aims the board into the glide zone, the middle of the top half of the wave. Too high and the wave will pass by. Too low and the wave could crash down on the little pug.

Timing matters also. Too soon or too late and Gidget will miss the wave. At the perfect moment, Alecia pushes the back of the surfboard down so the tip of the board points up. Gidget braces herself. Alecia shoves the board forward as hard as she can.

The rest is up to the little pug.

Small but Mighty

Gidget does much more than stand on the surfboard. Her little paws are in constant motion, dancing under her barrel body to maintain perfect balance. She doesn't have a lot of weight to throw around, just fifteen pounds, but she makes the most of it. She subtly shifts from right to left to turn the board. She adjusts forward and back as the water moves beneath her. Her head is pretty heavy, so she stretches it out like a turtle and swings it right and left, constantly making microadjustments to stay balanced.

When chop jostles the board, Gidget braces herself, legs spread wide.

The Physics of Surfing

A dog standing in the center of a board will remain afloat in still water if their buoyancy is greater than the downward force of gravity. But in the waves, the water beneath the board is constantly in motion.

When a wave approaches, the water rises until the board is tilted on a slope. Gravity pulls the board downslope, just like a sled.

There is a new force exerted by moving liquid called hydrodynamic force. This force pushes the board forward but also causes the board to want to turn. This rotational force is called torque. To stay balanced, a surfing dog has to create torque in the opposite direction to cancel out this rotational force. To adjust toward the right, Gidget has to shift her weight back and toward the right side. To adjust left, she shifts back and left.

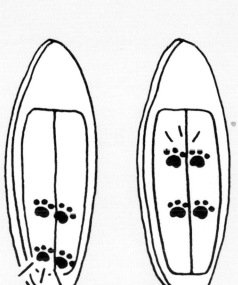

Slower   Faster

Gidget also controls her speed. Moving backward on the board creates drag, slowing the board down. Inching forward increases the speed. Like any surfer, the pug has to position herself just right to stay on the board. Too far forward and she might nosedive!

Wipeout!

Every surfer wipes out, and Gidget is no exception. Experienced surfing dogs don't mind one bit. They doggie-paddle to shore or are plucked out of the water by a nearby human. "But it's essential that all the dogs wear life jackets," says Alecia.

Play by the Rules

In dog surfing competitions, dogs first compete in their size categories. As a fifteen pounder, Gidget qualifies as a small or extra-small dog. Dogs are grouped into heats, with each heat lasting ten minutes. Judges score each dog's top three rides, looking for confidence and style, the length of the ride, and any tricks like turning on the board.

Fair play is also required. The dog closest to a breaking wave has possession and the right to surf that wave without interference. Owners are not allowed to position themselves in a way that blocks other surfers from riding a wave; they have to yield to a dog with possession (already surfing a wave), and they have to be careful not to launch their dogs into other dogs.

The winner of each size category gets a gold medal— and the chance to surf against the other winners for the title of Best in Surf.

Competition Ready

When they arrived at the beach for her first competition, Gidget unleashed a storm of yelps and squeaks. She wanted to do everything at once: run with other dogs, chase a ball, sprint into the water.

Alecia scooped her up, dotted sunscreen on her nose and ears, and wrestled her into a wet suit, as Gidget jabbered away: *ra, ra, reeee, ree, warrr, ree.*

But as soon as Alecia buckled Gidget's life jacket, the pug became calm and alert, her game face on.

After just three months of training, Gidget surfed like a champ. She won third place in the small dog category. It looked like the little pug had a great surfing future ahead of her.

But then something
went very wrong.

So Sick

Over the next few weeks, Gidget seemed tired. She began losing weight, slowly at first and then drastically. So they gave up surfing. The vet tried various blood tests but found nothing. The little pug began sleeping all day and wasted away until she looked like a skeleton. "We were really worried she wouldn't make it," Alecia says.

Finally, the vet figured out that Gidget had a disease of the pancreas found in humans, cats, and dogs: exocrine pancreatic insufficiency (EPI). Gidget's treatments began. Alecia added a special powder to her food, and Gidget slowly regained weight. Little by little, her energy returned.

She started scampering around, chasing balls and bugging Izzy to play again. "It's a miracle, really," says Alecia. "Most dogs with this disease are never very active again, but Gidgie recovered fully."

Gidget will need to take medicine for the rest of her life, but that doesn't stop her.

As soon as she was feeling better, she returned to the waves, taking the sport of dog surfing by storm.

Surf against Dogs Your Own Size

At a recent Surf Dog Surf-A-Thon, extra-small dogs are up first. Alecia checks out the waves, squinting into the fog. "I hope the judges will be able to see everyone," she says. "It's looking churny, like a washing machine. Not the best conditions for little dogs."

At the horn, the heat begins.

wAAOOONk!

Carson is the first up, in a crouch as he catches a short ride.

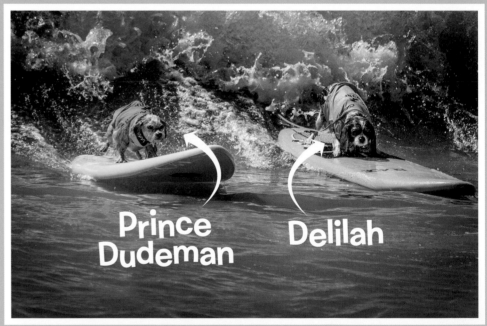

Prince Dudeman and Delilah grab a wave at the same time before tipping and tumbling off.

Gidget and Alecia head farther out, searching for a bigger wave. And she's off—surfing backward! She turns . . . and turns again . . . and rides all the way to the beach.

YAYYY!

Amazing!

WAAOOONK!

Alecia scoops up Gidget and hustles back into the breakers. They grab another good ride. There's less than a minute left. They need a third great ride to win. Out of the distance comes a little pink-and-white bundle. It's Gidget! A side-swell lifts and jostles the board. Gidget spreads her legs, lowers her head, and surfs all the way to beach.

The heat is over.

Back on the beach, Gidget runs around sniffing bags for food. Alecia
towels her off and bundles her up in a blanket. And they wait for the judges to
calculate the scores.

And the winner is . . .

Gidget!

She caught the smoothest wave, surfed the longest runs, executed
360-degree turns, AND held on through a tricky cross swell! The little pug wins
not only a gold medal, but also a coveted spot in the Best in Surf competition.

Surfing Together

Next up: the freestyle heats. This category includes multiple dogs on the same board and dogs and humans surfing together. Two doodles, Teddy and Derby, share a board and a love for the water. Whenever they get to shore, they leap off the board and bound back into the waves. Homer and his dog, Skyler, carve up some big, beautiful open faces. Hanzo, a boxer, surfs with eight-year-old Hugo and their dad.

Gidget hits the waves with her tandem partner, the curly-haired Prince Dudeman. Dudeman mostly stays still in the front, which adds some stability. It also means that Gidget has to account for his weight and positioning as she moves around the board. But they make a perfect pair, proudly surfing wave after wave.

Skyler

Hanzo

Surfing with the Big Dogs

The grand finale is the Best in Surf competition. Gidget stands alert, as Alecia and their friend Fiona study the waves. The wind picks up. "Conditions are changing rapidly," the MC announces. "It's going to be hard to find a clean, unbroken wave out there."

Finally, it's time. "Competitors, are you ready? You will have ten minutes . . . starting NOW!"

wAAOOONK! the horn blares.

Gidget sprints to the water and skitters to the front of the board as if she can't get out there fast enough. "Gidgie, back here," Alecia calls as she fights the white water.

Turbo, the golden, gets out to the waves quickly, turns, and gets a good stable ride in. A yellow Lab, Charlie, grabs a swell too, tail wagging slowly back and forth like a royal wave. Faith, a pit bull mix, starts a ride and tumbles off the board.

Charlie

Alecia heads out farther to where only the biggest waves break. Going out past the breakers means a smooth wave face and a long ride, but it also means that Alecia is in over her head. She has to tread water to keep afloat, navigate the swells, and keep Gidget on the board—all while looking to the horizon for an ideal wave.

Finally, one rises up and Alecia launches Gidget. The pug crouches faced forward, spins and faces back, pirouettes and faces forward again. It's the longest ride so far.

Sugar, a sweet white mutt, and her owner make their way even farther out. They try wave after wave, but the breakers are big and Sugar nosedives into the water again and again.

As the ten minutes wind down, Gidget joins Sugar far out in the ocean, both awaiting the perfect wave.

With less than a minute left, a wave approaches with a bigger wave looming behind it. Alecia launches Gidget onto the second wave, the monster. It surges forward—and swallows up the wave in front. It's a double-up! The peak grows and grows and Gidget's board rises and rises higher and higher. Suddenly the pug sails over the edge. She's in free fall. But she hangs on. The board lands with a slap, white water frothing all around.

Gidget twirls a 360 as if to say, "Look what I did!" and keeps going. She spots Fiona and barks out a joyous *rarrrrararar!*

Fiona grins, points to shore, and yells, "Take it home!"

The pug continues on and on, all the way to the beach. The crowd goes wild.

It was, by far, the longest ride of the day, and the one with the most pizzazz.

Alecia and Fiona are buoyant, cheering and praising the pug. Gidget wags her curly tail.

Was it the winning ride?

"Only ten seconds left," the MC calls. "Nine, eight, seven, six, five, four . . ."

Suddenly a huge wave rises up right behind Sugar.

"Three . . ." yells the MC.

Sugar and her board turn to shore.

"Two . . ."

Sugar takes off on the wave.

wAAOOONK!

Sugar beats the horn and rides down the massive face at a perfect slicing angle. Halfway to the beach, her board tilts and she tumbles into the water.

No one knows what to think. Gidget had the longest ride of the day with lots of fancy turns. Sugar rode the biggest, cleanest wave, but made it only halfway to the beach.

Who will win Best in Surf?

Sugar

The dogs and their humans gather at the award stage.

The enthusiastic tandem dog duo Teddy and Derby take third in the freestyle competition.

Gidget and Prince Dudeman win second.

And the pup and peep, Skyler and Homer take first place.

Finally, the big moment arrives—who will be crowned Best in Surf? The people quiet down around the podium. The dogs snooze, dig in the sand, or roll over for a belly rub.

Third place goes to . . . Turbo, the most consistent surfer in the heat.

Second goes to . . . Gidget, with the longest rides and most turns.

And first place, for the big wave at the bell . . . Sugar!

"Gidget did great," Alecia says proudly. The pug seems pretty happy with the outcome too. She noses around in her gift basket, pulls out a squeaky red bone, and holds it up like a trophy.

Alecia scoops her up and hugs her.

Gidget answers with a little lick.

Because they both know that *this* is what dog surfing is all about.

Going for Gold

Since her recovery, Gidget has become a world-champion surfer, winning many awards:

Best in Surf/Top Dog Champion
Gold Medal World Dog Surfing Championships
Gold Medal Imperial Beach Surf Dog
Silver Medal Surf Dog Surf-A-Thon
Silver Medal Purina Incredible Dog Challenge (twice)
Bronze Medal Purina Incredible Dog Challenge
Bronze Medal Huntington Beach Surf City Surf Dog

Best in Surf/Tandem
Silver Medal World Dog Surfing Championships

Small Dog Category
First Place World Dog Surfing Championships (twice)
First Place Surf Dog Surf-A-Thon (twice)
First Place Imperial Beach Surf Dog
Second Place Purina Incredible Dog Challenge (twice)
Second Place Surf Dog Surf-A-Thon
Second Place Unleashed by Petco Surf Dog Competition
Third Place Purina Incredible Dog Challenge
Third Place Surf Dog Surf-A-Thon

Small Dog Category/Tandem
Second Place World Dog Surfing Championships
Second Place Surf Dog Surf-A-Thon

William

World champion adaptive surfer
Dani Burt

Giving Back

While the team has been surfing to win, Gidget also surfs to raise money for humane societies, pug rescues, and other dog nonprofits. Having pulled through hard times of her own, Gidget surfs with kids and soldiers who have suffered trauma. "Sharing a board with Gidget builds confidence while they're having fun," says Alecia.

Team Gidget works to clean up the beach as well. While training, Alecia and Gidget have had to dodge floating plastic bottles and other trash. So they walk the beaches, picking up garbage whenever they can. They even made a free game for iTunes, called Surf Gidget the Pug, where Gidget surfs and snow sleds and picks up trash as she goes. "We hope that everyone who plays gets in the habit of picking up real trash too," says Alecia.

Hunter

Talking Trash

The Great Pacific Garbage Patch, an area of floating trash in the Pacific Ocean three times the size of France, has about 1.8 trillion pieces of rubbish in it. That's roughly 250 pieces for every human in the world.

Most of the garbage (80 percent) comes from trash on land that has been swept or dumped into the sea. Almost all of it—99.9 percent—is plastic. While an apple core and cardboard will decompose in the ocean in about 2 months, a plastic grocery bag will take 10 to 20 years and a plastic bottle will take 450 years.

Many plastics don't wear down; they just break into tinier and tinier pieces, turning the ocean into plastic soup. Marine animals and humans that eat seafood can ingest the microplastics and other toxins from the garbage.

Do your part to prevent this problem by reducing your use of plastic, reusing and recycling when possible, and properly disposing of all garbage you create or find, especially near the beach.

Learn more about the problem and clean-up efforts at TheOceanCleanup.com/great-pacific-garbage-patch.

The Real Winners

While Gidget continues to rack up medals, for her and Alecia it's no longer about the awards. "We are so blessed that Gidget is able to surf at all," says Alecia. "I started thinking there has to be a reason she recovered, a deeper meaning behind her surfing." These days, surfing is about the fun, the bond between them, the joy of movement—and about what they can do with Gidget's fame to make the world a better place. "Going forward we really want to focus on charity events and the environment," says Alecia. "And cherish our precious time together."

Don + Sampson

Carson + Jill

Alecia
+
Gidget

Kentucky
+
Derby

Asako
+
Koa
+
Lee

Safe Surfing

- You must be fit and a strong swimmer to spend any time in the surf.

- All dogs must wear life jackets.

- Check the surf forecast to make sure you will not be overpowered by large, crushing waves.

- Avoid surfing near obstacles such as rocks, cliffs, and piers.

- Wear sunscreen and stay hydrated.

- Don't surf alone, but make sure you have enough room to avoid being hit by someone else's board.

- Keep an eye on the waves at all times so you are not taken by surprise by sneaker waves.

- Avoid shore breaks, where waves close out powerfully onto the beach.

- Know your limits and stop before you or your dog are too tired.

Resist Longshore Currents

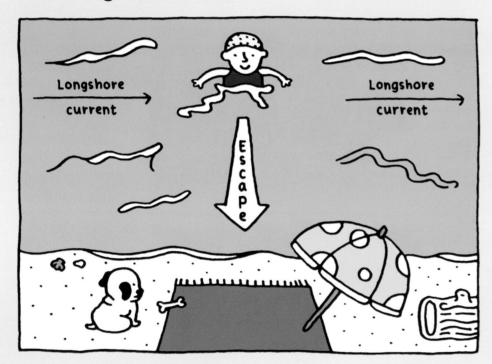

To avoid being pulled along the beach from a longshore current, find a spot on the beach and resist the side current to stay aligned with it. If necessary, leave the water and walk back to your starting point.

Escape Rip Currents

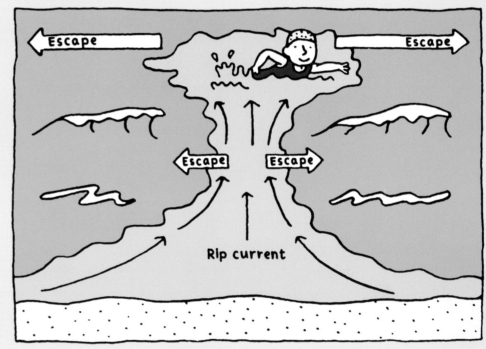

If you get caught in a rip current that pulls you out to sea, don't try to swim straight to shore. Swim parallel to the beach until you emerge from the rip current, then swim to shore.

Resources

Catch a Contest

Check out a dog surfing competition at one of these annual events:

Duke's OceanFest Going to the Dogs SurFUR ComPETition (Kuhio Beach, Hawaii)
DukesOceanFest.com

Florida Dog Surfing Championship (Cocoa Beach, Florida)
Sponsored by the East Coast Dog Surfing Association

Noosa Festival of Surfing (Australia)
NoosaFestivalofSurfing.com

Ohana Dog Surfing Competition (Galveston, Texas)
Sponsored by Ohana Surf & Skate and the Galveston Island Humane Society

Pups and SUPs Surfing Contest (St. Augustine, Florida)
VisitStAugustine.com/Event/Pups
-and-SUPs-Surfing-Contest

St. Lucie Dog Surf Classic (Pepper Park Beach, Florida)
Sponsored by the East Coast Dog Surfing Association

Surf Dog (Imperial Beach and Huntington Beach, California)
SurfDogEvents.com

Surf Dog Surf-A-Thon (Del Mar Beach, California)
AnimalCenter.org/Surf-Dog-Surf-a
-Thon

Surfing Dog Championships (Australia)
VetShopAustralia.com.au/Surfing
-Dog-Championships-C316.aspx

World Dog Surfing Championships (Linda Mar Beach, California)
SurfDogChampionships.com

Read More

Surfing Illustrated: A Visual Guide to Wave Riding by John Robison (McGraw-Hill, 2010)

Surf Science: An Introduction to Waves and Surfing by Tony Butt (University of Hawai'i Press, 2014)

Tracking Trash: Flotsam, Jetsam, and the Science of Ocean Motion by Loree Griffin Burns (Houghton Mifflin Harcourt, 2010)

Surf More

Follow Gidget online and on social media.
Facebook: Surf Gidget the Pug
Instagram: surf_gidget_the_pug
Twitter: GidgetsFanPage
Website: SurfGidget.com

Learn more about dog agility and the rules of competition.
AKC.org/Sports/Agility/Getting
-Started
USDAA.com/RulesReg.cfm

Read a great article about surfing science.
Exploratorium.edu/TheWorld/Surfing
/Physics/Index.html

Learn more about the Pacific garbage patch and efforts to clean it up.
NationalGeographic.org/encyclopedia
/great-pacific-garbage-patch
TheOceanCleanup.com/great-pacific
-garbage-patch

Sharing the Stoke

Alecia Nelson, thank you so much for sharing your love of Gidget and the sport of dog surfing with me. Going out into the waves with you and your adorable and feisty little pug was SICK (surfer slang for amazing). Fiona Kempin, thanks for helping bring it home! I'm also sincerely grateful to all the generous dog owners who so warmly welcomed this book and agreed to be involved.

The talented photographers Mike Barton, Charmaine Gray, Dominique Labrecque, Dale Porter, and Chris Stone made this book possible. Your photos made me laugh and smile every time I looked at them and have made this book so visually splendid.

A huge shout-out to photo editor, creative consultant, and friend Karin Anderson, who reviewed thousands of photos and offered a lively vision for the book. I love collaborating with you.

Christy Cox, I am so grateful to call you editor and friend. Thank you for sticking with me through the thorny process of finding the right story to tell. I think we got a great one! Thanks to Rob Casey, owner of Salmon Bay Paddle and author of *Stand Up Paddling: Flatwater to Surf and Rivers*, for reviewing surfing terminology.

Many thanks, too, for the good council and great feedback from writers Addie Boswell, Melissa Dalton, Ruth Feldman, Elizabeth Goss, Ellen Howard, Barbara Kerley, Amber Keyser, Michelle McCann, Sara Ryan, Nicole Schreiber, and Emily Whitman, and to designer Tony Ong, for pulling everything together so beautifully.

Finally, thanks to my mom and dad for introducing me to the joy of dogs and waves, and to Craig, Cobi, Izzi, and our dog, Reba, for making every beach day special.

—Elizabeth Rusch

ELIZABETH RUSCH has published more than a hundred magazine articles for children and adults and more than fifteen award-winning books for young readers, including *Avalanche Dog Heroes: Piper and Friends Learn to Search the Snow*; *The Next Wave: The Quest to Harness the Power of the Oceans*; *The Mighty Mars Rovers: The Incredible Adventures of Spirit and Opportunity*; *Electrical Wizard: How Nikola Tesla Lit Up the World*; and the graphic novel *Muddy Max: The Mystery of Marsh Creek*. Her work has been honored by the Junior Library Guild, the American Library Association, *School Library Journal*, *Kirkus*, the Subaru Prize, NBC News, the Oregon Book Award, Washington Reads, and the New York Public Library. Elizabeth, her husband, their teen children, and their quirky dog Reba all enjoy playing in the waves on the Oregon Coast.